Modern Rhymes About Ancient Times

ANCIENT GREECE

Written by Susan Altman and Susan Lechner

Illustrated by Deborah Schilling

Children's Press®
A Division of Scholastic Inc.
New York • Toronto • London • Auckland • Sydney
Mexico City • New Delhi • Hong Kong
Danbury, Connecticut

TROJAN HORSE, OLYMPIC GAMES,

Comic plays and complex names.

Aesop's fables, Marathon,

Socrates, and Parthenon.

Cradle of democracy,

Drama, and philosophy.

The many gods of ancient times—

They're all here when you

Read these rhymes.

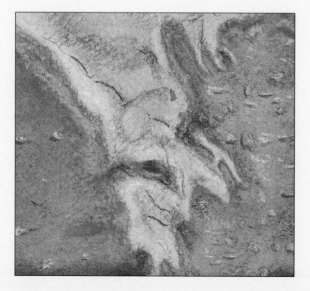

To Robin and Lee—my own nominees for Greek goddesses.—S. R. A.

To Florence and Howard, Eric and Allison, Dana and Dave—my special extended family.—S. L.

Reading Consultant: Nanci Vargus, Ed.D., Decatur Township Schools, Indianapolis, Indiana

Book production by Editorial Directions, Inc.

Book design by Marie O'Neill

Library of Congress Cataloging-in-Publication Data
Altman, Susan.
    Ancient Greece / written by Susan Altman and Susan Lechner ; illustrated by Deborah Schilling.
        p. cm. — (Modern rhymes about ancient times)
        Includes bibliographical references and index.
        ISBN 0-516-21150-1 (lib. bdg.)   0-516-27373-6 (pbk.)
        1. Greece—Juvenile poetry. 2. History, Ancient—Juvenile poetry. 3. Children's poetry, American. [1. Greece—Civilization—To 146 B.C.—Poetry. 2. American poetry.] I. Lechner, Susan. II. Schilling, Deborah, ill. III. Title. IV. Series.
    PS3551.L7943 A845 2001
    811'.54—dc21   2001028262

TABLE OF CONTENTS

Pronouncing Greek Names . . . 4

The Greek Alphabet 6

Solon 8

Aesop's Fables 9

The Battle of Marathon 10

The Philosopher Socrates . . . 12

Hippocrates 13

The Parthenon 14

Greek Columns 16

Pericles 18

Diogenes 19

Aristophanes 20

Herodotus, the Father
    of History 21

Demosthenes 22

Aristotle 24

Archimedes 25

The Agora 26

Let's Eat! 28

Childhood in Sparta 30

Olympic Games 32

Trojan Horse 34

The Gordian Knot 36

Zeus 38

The Myth of the Minotaur . . 40

The Myth of the Fates 42

The Myth of Medusa 43

The Iliad and Odyssey 44

More About
    Ancient Greece 46

Index 47

PRONOUNCING GREEK NAMES

Many Greek names end in "-es."
Say it as if it were "eez."
If you do this, you'll find it's no problem,
To say them is really a breeze.

Many Greek names are really quite long.
It will help if you all comprehend,
The accent will fall almost always
Three syllables down from the end.

For instance:
There's Heracles, (HAIR-uh-kleez)
Also Euripides, (yoo-RIP-uh-deez)
Quite brilliant Socrates, (SOCK-ra-tees)
And Aristophanes. (air-is-TOF-ah-neez)

Just follow these rules
And you'll rarely go wrong.
You'll be able to say with great glee,
"If you want to know someone
Who speaks perfect Greek,
Just sit back and listen to me!"

Heracles

Euripides

Socrates

Aristophanes

THE GREEK ALPHABET

Alpha, beta, gamma, delta,
That's the way it starts.
Epsilon, zeta, theta, eta
Follow on the charts.

Iota, kappa, and then lambda,
Mu, nu, and xi.
Omicron, pi, rho, and sigma,
Tau, upsilon, phi.

Chi, psi, and last, omega.
Now we're finally done.
Try it out loud. Say it faster.
Talking Greek is fun!

This is how you pronounce the Greek alphabet: *alpha* (AL-fuh), *beta* (BAY-tuh), *gamma* (GAM-uh), *delta* (DELL-tuh), *epsilon* (EPP-sill-on), *zeta* (ZAY-tuh), *theta* (THAY-tuh), *eta* (AY-tuh), *iota* (eye-OH-tuh), *kappa* (CAP-uh), *lambda* (LAMB-duh), *mu* (MOO), *nu* (NOO), *xi* (ZYE), *omicron* (OH-mick-ron), *pi* (PYE), *rho* (ROW), *sigma* (SIG-muh), *tau* (TAW), *upsilon* (UP-sill-on), *phi* (FYE), *chi* (KYE), *psi* (SYE), and *omega* (oh-MAY-guh).

A· Alpha
Β Beta
Γ Gamma
Δ Delta

SOLON

(About 630–560 B.C.)

Solon was wise; Solon was fair—
The ruler Athens needed.
He made good laws; he helped the poor.
His wise reforms succeeded.

He gave the poor the right to vote,
Demanded courts be just.
The "Father of Democracy,"
He earned the people's trust.

Solon is pronounced SOLE-un.

AESOP'S FABLES (Late sixth century B.C.)

"The Boy and the Wolf,"
"The Fox and the Grapes,"
You've read them in books.
You've seen them on tapes.

Written by Aesop—
An ancient Greek slave.
They each have a lesson
On how to behave.

His dozens of fables
Have morals so true
That though they're quite old,
They sound just like new.

Aesop is pronounced EE-sop.

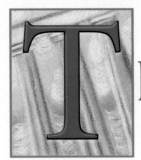THE BATTLE OF MARATHON (490 B.C

The Athenians and the Persians
Could never get along.
Each accused the other
Of doing something wrong.

Their armies met at Marathon—
A flat and grassy plain.
Any hopes they had for peace
Were totally in vain.

Athens won the battle,
But how to send the news?
Back then there was no CNN,
With handy TV crews.

Athens was 26 miles away.
"I'll get there!" a brave soldier cried.
He ran all the way without making a stop,
Told the people—then fell down and died!

Today it's a race
With a blistering pace,
With runners from Maine to Seattle.
The Marathon run
(Hardest under the sun)
Is named for this ancient Greek battle.

THE PHILOSOPHER SOCRATES (470–399 B.C.)

Socrates, the thinker,
Asked questions all day long—
What is goodness? What is truth?
Why do folks go wrong?

He questioned all authority,
And though his speech was mild,
His teachings were so radical,
He drove the rulers wild.

They said he led the young astray
And sentenced him to death.
He didn't ask for mercy.
He didn't waste his breath.

They said he must drink poison.
His friends were at his side.
He took the cup of hemlock*,
He drank, and bravely died.

*Hemlock is a poisonous drink made from the hemlock plant.

HIPPOCRATES (460—377 B.C.)

Father of modern medicine,
Hippocrates led the way.
His skillful treatment blazed the trail
For doctors of today.

While other ancient doctors
Relied on superstition,
He based his care on proven facts
And counseled good nutrition.

In tribute to Hippocrates,
Today our doctors swear
An oath to treat their patients well
And give the best of care.

"I will lead my life and practice my art in uprightness and honor."
—From the Hippocratic oath

THE PARTHENON

They chipped at the marble.
They did it by hand.
The work they created
Was brilliant and grand.

With glorious columns,
Carved horses and men,
Goddesses, chariots,
Battles . . . and then

They put them together
On top of a hill.
The Parthenon temple
Stood proudly and still.

You can see it today
Many centuries later.
Some say there has never
Been anything greater.

GREEK COLUMNS

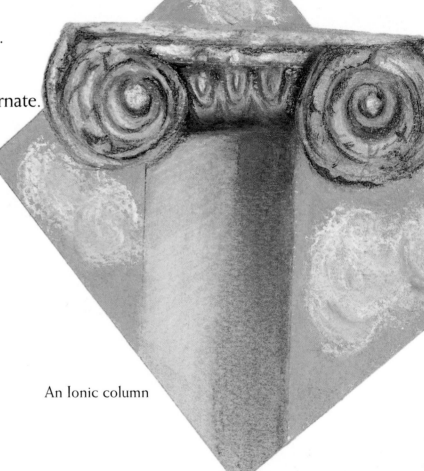

Ionic columns are topped with scrolls.

Doric columns are flat.

Corinthian columns are much more ornate.

And now you know all about that.

An Ionic column

Ionic is pronounced eye-ON-ik. *Doric* is pronounced DOOR-ik. *Corinthian* is pronounced core-IN-thee-un. These types of columns are still used today. Some of the columns on the White House are Ionic.

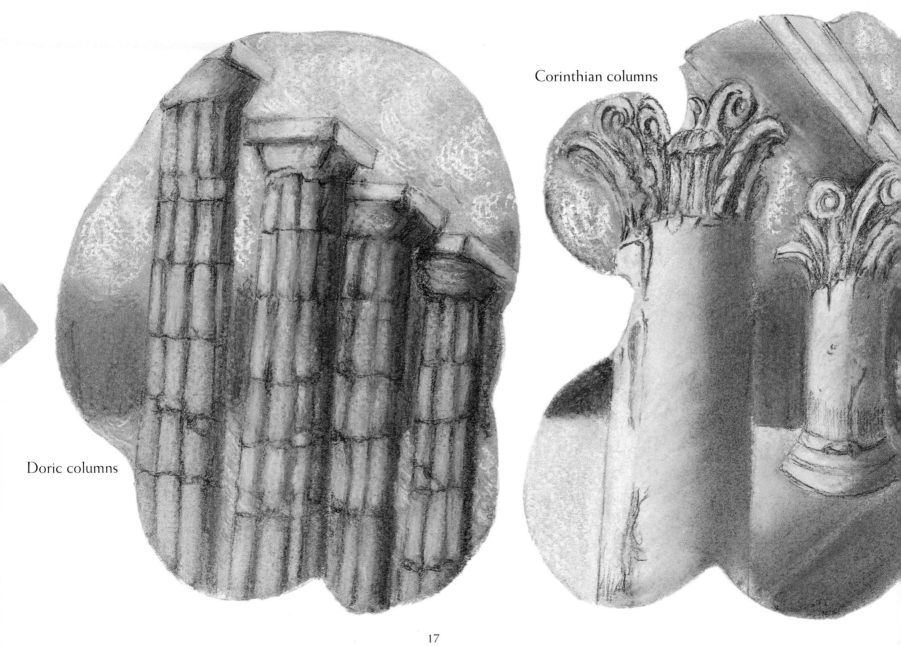

Corinthian columns

Doric columns

PERICLES (about 495—429 B.C.)

Pericles, the statesman,
Pericles, the sage,
Pericles ruled Athens
In its Golden Age.

He beautified the city
And gave the people power.
Pericles led Athens
To its finest hour.

Pericles is pronounced PEAR-ih-kleez.

IOGENES (412—323 B.C.)

People cheat!
People lie!
This made Diogenes sad.
He wanted to prove,
If just to himself,
That everyone wasn't so bad.

"But how can I do this?"
He thought to himself.
And then he came up with a plan.
He'd look through the city,
A lamp in his hand,
In search of just one honest man.

His plan didn't work,
Though he searched day and night.
(He searched in the cold and the heat.)
He was always quite poor.
He refused any help.
(He lived in a tub in the street.)

Diogenes is pronounced dye-AH-gen-eez.

19

ARISTOPHANES

(About 445—385 B.C.)

Aristophanes was funny

And he made a lot of money

Writing comedies all Athens went to see.

Making fun of politicians,

Teachers, writers, and physicians,

He wrote better stuff than what's now on TV.

Aristophanes is pronounced air-is-TOF-ah-neez.

HERODOTUS, THE FATHER OF HISTORY

(about 484—425 B.C.)

"The Father of History,"
That's what he's called.
Important events
He described and recalled.

He wrote about Persia;
He wrote about Greece;
He wrote about wars;
He wrote about peace.

Herodotus told us
A lot that we know
About things that happened
A long time ago.

Herodotus is pronounced hih-RAD-uh-tus.

DEMOSTHENES (384—322 B.C.)

He had an awful stutter,

He'd just mumble, halt, and mutter

Whenever he was called upon to speak.

People laughed at him and teased him

Till humiliation seized him.

Yes, Demosthenes was one unhappy Greek.

So he practiced public speaking.

He tried yelling, howling, shrieking.

He tried talking when his mouth was full of stones.

He would shout while he was running

And his progress was quite stunning.

Yes, Demosthenes had come into his own.

Demosthenes is pronounced duh-MAHS-thuh-neez.

He alerted Greece of danger
That was coming from a stranger—
A warning—and he had to pass it on.
With a voice quite clear and steady
He told people to be ready
For invasion by the King of Macedon.

He no longer had a stutter,
Or a mumble, or a mutter.
People listened now when he got up to speak.
He came through when he was needed,
And his warning words were heeded.
Yes, Demosthenes was one heroic Greek.

ARISTOTLE (384 B.C.—322 B.C.)

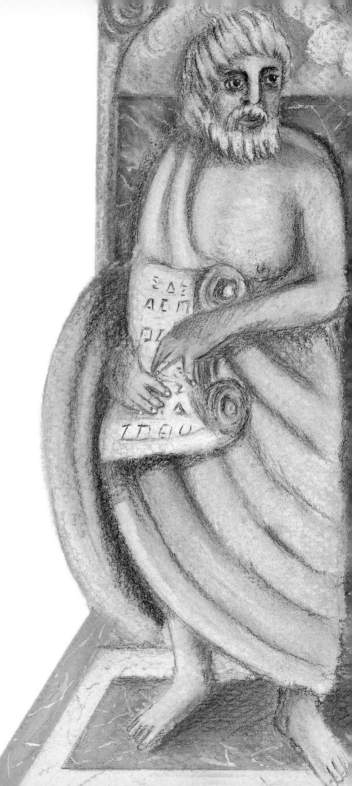

Philosopher and scientist,

Teacher and biologist,

Aristotle fit no simple mold.

A writer and a critic,

He was always analytic.

And his thinking was more valuable than gold.

Aristotle is pronounced AIR-is-tot-uhl.

# ARCHIMEDES (About 287–212 B.C.)

Bright Archimedes,
Brilliant Greek scientist,
Sat and relaxed in his bath.
He studied the water,
And what he discovered
Set scientists on a new path.

He saw that an object,
When placed in the water,
Always displaced its own weight.
He shouted, "Eureka!"
Which means, "I have found it!"
Then dried off and felt really great.

Archimedes is pronounced ark-uh-ME-deez.
Eureka is pronounced yoo-REE-kah.

 # THE AGORA

There are no malls
Just shopping stalls
At the agora.

Buy what you wish
From bread to fish
At the agora.

Come hear the news
And latest views
At the agora.

Part marketplace,
Part meeting space—
That's the agora.

Agora is pronounced AG-or-uh.

LET'S EAT!

Food was quite simple in ancient Greece;
Most folks ate two meals a day.
Mid-morning, some beans with a turnip
    or two
Served in a bowl made of clay.

The main meal came later, in mid-afternoon,
With more on the table to eat.
Some olives and figs, served with fresh bread and cheese—
And maybe a small piece of meat.

CHILDHOOD IN SPARTA

Living in Sparta was tough.
Life was brutal and rigid and rough.

Young boys were trained early to fight,
Forbidden to read or to write.

They slept on some mats on the floor.
Their whole life was training for war.

They often were hungry and cold.
Their elders thought this made them bold.

I'm sure that we can all agree,
That Sparta was no place to be.

OLYMPIC GAMES

Every four years
All wars would cease;
Olympic Games
Were held in Greece.

Honored athletes
Raced and jumped,
Bodies straining,
Muscles pumped.

One special note,
As history shows,
None of the athletes
Wore any clothes.

The modern Olympic Games were revived in 1896. Nearly all the countries in the world participate.

ROJAN HORSE

This story is
A famous one.
It's one that you should know,
About deceit
And trickery
That happened long ago.

It seems the Greeks
And Trojans
Were in a nasty fight.
The sturdy walls
Surrounding Troy
Could challenge dynamite!

The Greeks were stumped.
What should they do?
They all were mystified.
How could they win
The battle if
They couldn't get inside?

And so they built
A giant horse
To fool the folks of Troy.
Who'd think it was
A gift for them—
A great big wooden toy.

The Trojans were the people who lived in Troy.

The Greeks then brought
The wooden horse
And left it by the gate.
The Trojans dragged
The horse inside
And thus they sealed their fate.

Hidden in
The horse were Greeks,
Who opened up the door.
They let their fellow
Soldiers in
And won the Trojan War.

THE GORDIAN KNOT

Old King Gordius tied such a knot
That no one could ever untie it.
Though people would travel from all over Greece
To ask for a chance just to try.

According to legend, the man who untied it
Would rule over vast foreign lands.
(That's why the attempt to unravel the knot
Attracted so many Greek hands.)

Then young Alexander (later "the Great")
Said, "Stand back, and watch what I do."
And unlike the others, he picked up his sword,
And decisively cut the knot through.

Do you think this was cheating?
Or was he just clever?
Students will argue
This question forever.

ZEUS

Mighty Zeus was king of the gods.
Poseidon ruled the sea.
Hades ruled the underworld.
They were the reigning three.

Zeus controlled the weather,
With power, good and bad!
He'd throw his mighty thunderbolts
Whenever he got mad.

Though mighty Zeus was king of gods
Revered all over Greece,
His wife, the goddess Hera,
Would never give him peace.

Whenever Zeus was gone too long,
His wife would fume and fuss,
'Cause back in Greece, the ancient gods
Had problems, just like us.

Zeus is pronounced zooss. *Poseidon* is pronounced puh-SYE-dun.
Hades is pronounced HAY-deez.

THE MYTH OF THE MINOTAUR

The Minotaur was a monster
With nasty personal habits.
A man with a head of a bull,
He ate people as if they were rabbits.

To keep him relaxed and quite cheerful
(They didn't have antidepressants),
Each nine years, the people would feed him
A meal of fourteen adolescents.

He lived in a maze called a labyrinth
(According to this ancient fable).
The Minotaur found it quite cozy
Though it hadn't been wired for cable.

Then Theseus entered the maze,
And though he expected resistance,
He took out his magical sword
And ended the monster's existence.

Theseus is pronounced THEE-see-us.

THE MYTH OF THE FATES

In peacetime and battle
Through silence and strife,
The Greeks often spoke of
The great "Thread of Life."

How long will you live?
And when will you die?
The Greeks thought these judgments
Were made from on high.

Three glinty-eyed goddesses
Known as "The Fates"
Made all those decisions,
Selecting the dates.

One Fate did the spinning.
One measured the thread.
And when the third cut it,
That's it—you were dead!

THE MYTH OF MEDUSA

Medusa had only bad hair days
'Cause snakes grew right out of her head.
They writhed, they slithered, they hissed, they coiled.
Medusa filled people with dread.

Medusa had one other problem:
It tended to keep her alone.
If people should happen to look at her face,
They instantly turned into stone.

THE ILIAD AND ODYSSEY

The Iliad and *The Odyssey* are books that you should read—

Tales of love and trickery, magic spells and greed.

Monsters, gods, and goddesses,

Lots of action too.

You'll find them in the library.

They're waiting there for you!

Iliad is pronounced IL-ee-id. *Odyssey* is pronounced OD-uh-see.

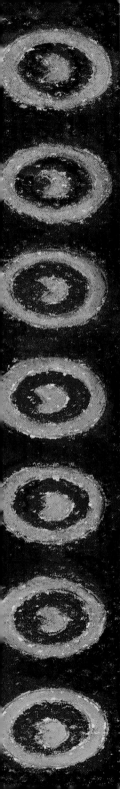

MORE ABOUT ANCIENT GREECE

Books

Bardi, Matilde, and John Malam. *Ancient Greece.* Chicago: NTC/Contemporary Publishing Co., 2000.

Blacklock, Dyan. *Pankration: The Ultimate Game.* Morton, Ill.: Albert Whitman & Co., 1999.

Greenblatt, Miriam. *Alexander the Great and Ancient Greece.* Woodbury, Conn.: Benchmark Books, 2000.

Hicks, Peter. *Ancient Greece.* Austin, Tex.: Raintree/Steck-Vaughn, 2000.

Websites

The Ancient Greek World Index
http://www.museum.upenn.edu/Greek_World/Index.html/
Find a thorough index of various aspects of the ancient Greek world on this University of Pennsylvania Museum website

Greek Civilization for Middle Schoolers
http://www.greekciv.pdx.edu/structure/carr2.html
Learn about sports, war, and politics from this Portland State University website

The Greeks
http://www.pbs.org/empires/thegreeks/
Explores the lives of ancient Greeks, including leaders and heroes, on this PBS website

History of the Olympic Games
http://www.usswim.org/olympics/olyhist.htm
Read about the history of the Olympic Games from the USA Swimming website

INDEX

Aesop, 9

Agora, 26

Alexander the Great, 37

alphabet, 6

Archimedes, 25

Aristophanes, 4, 20

Aristotle, 24

athletes, 32

Battle of Marathon, 10

Corinthian columns, 16

Demosthenes, 22–23

Diogenes, 19

Doric columns, 16

Euripides, 4

fables, 9

"The Fates," 42

food, 28

Golden Age, 18

Gordian knot, 36–37

Gordius, 36

Hades, 38

Hera, 38

Heracles, 4

Herodotus, 21

Hippocrates, 13

The Iliad, 44

Ionic columns, 16

Marathon, 10

marketplace, 26

medicine, 13

Medusa, 43

Minotaur, 40

myths, 40, 42, 43

names, 4

The Odyssey, 44

Olympic Games, 32

Parthenon temple, 14

Pericles, 18

philosophy, 12, 24

Poseidon, 38

religion, 38

science, 24, 25

Socrates, 4, 12

Solon, 8

Sparta, 30

sports, 32

Theseus, 40

"Thread of Life," 42

Trojan Horse, 34–35

Trojan War, 35

Troy, 34

Zeus, 38

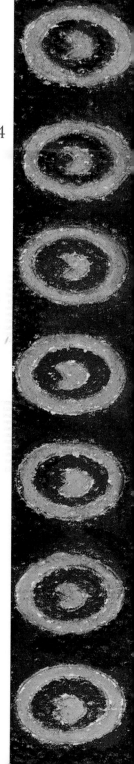

ABOUT THE AUTHORS

Susan Altman and **Susan Lechner**, both graduates of Wellesley College, currently produce the Emmy Award–winning television program *It's Academic* in Washington, D.C., and Baltimore, Maryland. They have also produced *It's Elementary, Heads Up!,* and *Pick Up the Beat.* They are coauthors of *Followers of the North Star* a book of rhymes for young people (also published by Children's Press). Ms. Altman is also the author of the play *Out of the Whirlwind* and the books *Extraordinary African-Americans* and *The Encyclopedia of African-American Heritage.*